BORN FREE FOUNDATION

Bear Rescue

True-Life Stories

D1017627

Bear Rescue

True-Life Stories

Written by
Jess French

We all feel deeply for little children when they become orphans. Even more when these children have no other family members to look after them and love them. But I wonder how often we realize this also happens to little animals.

Sometimes it is because the mother has been killed by hunters, or by another animal. Sometimes, as in this story, it is because of a natural disaster—the fearful flooding of a big river in Georgia which overwhelmed the landscape, separating families or causing death to many creatures that could not escape in time.

This story is a true one, about three bears. Not the famous three who discovered Goldilocks eating their porridge, but three little cubs (one on its own and two sisters). All three little bears were orphans—Louisa was separated from her mother as the violent surge of the rising water brought huge trees crashing to the ground. But the little sisters, Mollie and Georgia, had already moved to safety with their mother to find a new home on a different part of the mountain. Tragically, when their mother went off in search of food she was killed. By a poacher.

I am sure they will not have been the only little animals to have experienced this terrifying ordeal, and some will surely not have survived. But, as you will read in this touchingly written story, they were given a second chance in life.

I have never been to Georgia, but that doesn't mean I am indifferent to the tragedies that befall all living creatures. At The Born Free Foundation we are dedicated to trying to help animals—whether it is because they have become victims of natural disasters, or kept in very bad conditions in captivity. So, when we heard about the little bears from another charity—The Mayhew Animal Home—we knew we had to do something to help.

When the little cubs were rescued they were taken to Tbilisi's Animal Shelter, where they were only three of an overwhelming number of animals—mainly dogs and cats—who were also victims of the flood. They were kindly looked after, but it was vital that they were taken to a place that was more sympathetic to their wild nature.

This story will take you on their journey to Arcturos in northern Greece. Although I have known their story for a long time, it still moves me very much. Of course, for all kinds of reasons, we cannot always help—but we never give up trying. At Born Free there are no barriers—no borders—no creature to which we will not try to give a second chance in life. And I know the three bears have been given just that.

Virginia McKenna

Virginia McKenna OBE
Actress and Founder Trustee, Born Free Foundation

This is the true story of three young bears, Mollie, Georgia, and Louisa, who were born in the mountains in the Republic of Georgia. It's about the series of sad events that changed their lives forever, the challenges that faced their rescuers, and the fortunate circumstances that eventually brought the three cubs together.

Georgia FACTFILE

- Born in the wild in Tbilisi, Georgia in 2015
- Brave, feisty, and very protective of her sister
- Her best friend is her sister, Mollie
- Loves to walk in the mountains

Mollie FACTFILE

- Born in the wild in Tbilisi, Georgia in 2015
- Shy and scared of people, but can be tempted with honey and fruit!
- Her favorite food is watermelon
- Loves to roll in the grass

Louisa

FACTFILE

- Born in the wild in Tbilisi, Georgia in 2015
- Very nervous around other bears and people
- Her best friend is Patrick, another orphaned bear cub
- Her favorite food is berries

Chapter One

A cloud of black flies buzzed loudly as they circled the stinking rubbish heap. It was midday in Tbilisi, and you could almost see the stench, hanging in a green mist over the piles of waste. Without knowing she was there, it would be easy to miss the small, brown body, lying among the old newspapers, empty cans, and food wrappers. The young bear cub lay motionless on top of the rubbish heap, exhausted, starving, and dehydrated. This was no life for a baby bear, but it was the life that had been forced upon Louisa.

Tbilisi is the capital city of Georgia. Georgia is a country between Russia and Turkey.

In June 2015, the River Vere, which runs through Georgia, had flooded. When the floods came, Louisa had been learning to swim with her mother and brother. At first, all she noticed was the water level beginning to rise. Soon, the water started flowing faster and she found it very difficult to stay afloat.

Bears love water. Cubs are taught to swim by their mothers from a young age. They use water to cool off in the heat, hide their tracks, escape from flies, and hunt fish, frogs, and aquatic insects. They also seem to swim just for fun!

FACT FILE

Louisa's mother snorted loudly at her cubs. Louisa knew that that sound meant: *"DANGER!"* Louisa was paddling hard to catch up with her mother, when an unexpected current grabbed her and dragged her to the opposite bank. Her mother snorted again and again. Louisa tried as hard as she could to swim back across the river, but the water was too fast and too strong. Reluctantly, she climbed onto the bank and loped toward a nearby tree with low branches, watching her mother and brother do the same across the river.

FACT FILE

Adult European brown bears rarely make sounds, unless they are very frightened or communicating with their cubs. Mother bears are able to use lots of different noises in addition to body language to talk to their cubs, including moaning, grunting, growling, huffing, clacking their teeth, popping their jaws, and snorting.

From the other side of the river, Louisa's mother continued to snort at her. The sound let Louisa know that she was not totally alone. But as the roaring of the water grew louder, it eventually drowned out her mother's calls. Louisa was very scared. She closed her eyes and pushed her body into the tree trunk, anchoring her claws deep into the bark.

Moments later there was a thunderous crash from the other riverbank. The tree, which her mother and brother had climbed, had fallen into the river. The rushing water soon carried the tree far downstream and out of Louisa's sight. She clung to her tree, watching the water hurtle down the mountain. She was tired, hungry, and very frightened. She hung onto the tree until the sun set and the forest turned black. Then, finally, Louisa fell asleep.

There are eight different bear species: American black bear, brown bear, polar bear, Asiatic black bear, giant panda, sloth bear, sun bear, and Andean/spectacled bear.

The only bear that lives in Europe is the European brown bear, a subspecies of the brown bear. Other subspecies of brown bear include the grizzly bear.

FACT FILE

The next morning, Louisa's forest looked totally different. Many trees had fallen down and the earth was covered in a layer of gray sludge. She was still hungry, but at less than four months old, Louisa did not yet know which berries were good to eat, or how to hunt insects and small animals. She had always relied on her mother to catch fish for her and show her the best places to forage for blackberries. Still almost entirely dependent on her mother's milk, Louisa had only just started to learn how to find her own food. Now she was all alone.

FACT FILE

A mother bear weans her cubs at about five months of age. She begins to teach them which food is good to eat by letting them smell her breath.

Chapter Two

Trying to remember what her mother had taught her, Louisa sniffed the crisp mountain air. All of the smells were confused now, the sweet scent of berries lost in the sulfurous stench of floodwater and mud. Somewhere in the distance she thought that she could smell meat. So she followed her nose down the mountain, toward a human city.

She had never been this far downhill before. There were lots of food smells here, but there was also something else. Further upland, in the forest where

Louisa grew up, she had not encountered this scent often. But she knew what it was. Humans. On foraging trips through the forest with her mother and brother, Louisa had rarely seen humans. But when she did, her mother would send her scurrying into the cover of a bush. So Louisa knew that humans must be dangerous.

FACT FILE

A mother bear's number one priority is the safety and education of her cubs. She is often very strict; she knows that the training of her cubs is crucial to their survival, and they have lots to learn!

Eventually her aching belly left Louisa with little choice. If she did not eat something soon she would starve to death. As she approached the edge of the city, the stench of rotting fruit and rancid meat caught her nose. It didn't smell like the delicious fresh food that her mother had brought her, but it might be enough to stop her from starving. Louisa's excellent sense of smell led her to a huge rubbish heap on the outskirts of the city.

Louisa approached the rubbish cautiously, looking around for any signs of movement. When she was certain that there were no people close by, she began to rummage through crisp packets and carrier bags in search of food, occasionally eating bits of paper and plastic by accident in her rush to devour the little scraps she could find. The food was not tasty, but after days of eating nothing at all Louisa was grateful to have anything in her stomach. Just as she was beginning to relax, Louisa heard footsteps approaching. A *human!* She began digging frantically, burying herself in the rubbish, hoping not to be seen.

The human came close, but didn't spot the tip of Louisa's ears poking up between a crumpled magazine and a discarded coffee cup. The human threw a bag of rubbish on the heap and disappeared out of sight. When she was sure he was gone, Louisa clambered back to the top, her fur now sticky and wet from a lemonade that had spilled down her back.

In the wild, the European brown bear's diet consists of mainly berries, grasses, herbs, vegetables, and fungi. They also eat fish and other animals, when they can catch them. Animals like bears, that eat both vegetables and meat, are called omnivores.

It was not much of a life, but Louisa continued like this for what seemed like several weeks: eating just enough to survive, but not enough to thrive. In the beginning, she would climb out of the rubbish heap each day and wander through the streets, searching for anything edible. The biggest challenge was finding fresh water. In her mountain forest, she was never far from the cool and clear waters of a river or stream.

Now she had to make do with muddy puddles and overflowing drains. Louisa was constantly alert, always sniffing the air to check if humans were approaching. Whenever she smelled their scent she would run back to the rubbish heap and hide.

In the wild, bear cubs will stay with their mother for the first 18 to 36 months of their lives, only separating for short periods, such as when the mother bear is hunting or chasing away a predator. During this time, the mother bear will teach her cubs all the skills they need to survive alone, including how to hunt, dig, fish, and recognize danger.

FACT FILE

Soon she had so little energy that she would not leave the rubbish heap during the day. She was so weak that she could not even hide when humans came close. Every day she lost a little weight. Though she did not know it, without her mother's warmth and milk, Louisa would not make it through the winter.

Chapter Three

A couple of miles from Louisa's rubbish heap, further up the mountain, two more bear cubs were trying to adjust to life alone. During the floods, Mollie, Georgia, and their mother had been forced to move away from the area they had grown up in and onto another part of the mountain. Their home had been ruined and there was no longer any food there to eat. Their mother had seemed nervous about leading her cubs to this new habitat. There were fewer trees here and it reeked of a smell that the cubs did not yet know, but would later come to associate with humans.

Their mother left Mollie and Georgia in the hollow of an old, dead tree, while she went to find them some food. As they watched her large, hairy rump disappear, they rolled around in the grass, biting at each other's faces. Bear cubs love to play. If they had known this would be the last time they would ever see her, they might have watched more closely.

After a while, there was an enormous bang. This was a new sound to the cubs, but it was very frightening. They wished their mother would hurry up and return. They were starting to become very hungry and longed to snuggle into her fur, and fill their bellies with her rich, warm milk. As darkness fell, the cubs started to feel scared and called out to their mother, begging her to return. But she would not. Their mother had been killed by a poacher, who would sell her body parts on the black market.

Mollie and Georgia waited and waited. They did not like this new part of the mountain. It was eerily silent, no birds sang, and the smell of humans lingered in the air. Finally, the cubs realized that their mother was not coming back to them. With aching bellies, Mollie and Georgia, like Louisa, tried to forage for themselves. They did not want to stay in this new habitat, where their mother had disappeared. They could not return to the forest they had grown up in because the floods had destroyed most of the plants that Mollie and Georgia knew were safe to eat. So they had to use their own initiative. They too were drawn to the smells of Tbilisi.

Bears have one of the best senses of smell of all land mammals. They can smell meat from up to 20 miles (32 km) away.

Unlike Louisa, Mollie and Georgia wandered around in plain sight along the edge of a human road, scavenging on rubbish thrown from passing cars. They had never seen cars before and did not know that these metal boxes contained humans, whose smell they had become so frightened of. All the same, they jumped out of the way every time they heard the whoosh of a car as it zoomed past.

The bear cubs' presence did not go unnoticed. During the floods, many of the animals from Tbilisi Zoo had escaped. Some people driving past Mollie and Georgia began to wonder if these cubs might have run away from the zoo. Others were frightened that the bears would come down the mountain and into their homes.

It did not take long for the authorities in Tbilisi to be alerted to the presence of the bears. After some investigations, they realized that the cubs had not escaped from the zoo after all, but that they were wild bears. Everyone agreed that it was not safe for them to be left by the road. They could be injured by a car or starve to death through lack of food and milk. Tbilisi Municipal Animal Shelter offered to send their Emergency Response Services team to catch Mollie and Georgia and bring them to the safety of their center.

Bear milk contains three times the amount of energy that cow milk does. It contains over 20% fat and over 11% protein.

It was not an easy task, catching two terrified bear cubs. As the white van pulled up, Mollie and Georgia scampered up the mountain, away from the engine noise. As the doors of the van opened, the air was filled with the scent of humans. Mollie and Georgia recognized that smell. It was the smell of whatever killed their mother.

Adult brown bears can reach speeds of over 30 miles (48 km) per hour.

Mollie and Georgia ran from the men as fast as they could. Though they were only cubs and weak from their poor diets, the sisters were still surprisingly fast. Georgia was quicker than her sister, but would stop every so often to make sure that Mollie was still with her. Since their mother had died, the cubs had become closer than ever. Nothing would separate them. Suddenly, a human appeared in front of them. There had been a second vehicle, which had parked further up the hill without the bear cubs noticing. More humans were heading down the mountain toward them. The humans captured the bears as gently as they could, quickly loading them into the back of the van. Off to yet another new home.

Chapter Four

It was around the same time that Mollie and Georgia were rescued that Louisa stopped burying herself in the rubbish to hide from the humans. With no fresh water to drink, she was so dehydrated and weak that she could barely move at all. It didn't take long for the humans to notice her. They wondered if she was already dead, because she was so still.

When the white van arrived for her, Louisa had just enough energy to lift her head and watch as three men in uniforms jumped out. As the rescuers lifted her, she did not put up a fight. She was rigid with shock, and apart from the weak groan that echoed through her hollow chest as they pulled her from the heap, she gave no sign of life.

Louisa was taken to Tbilisi Municipal Animal Shelter, an isolated complex of buildings in the middle of a vast expanse of arid scrubland, near Lake Lisi. Despite its peaceful location, the shelter was a hive of activity. People rushed around the clinic with white masks on their faces. Everywhere you turned dogs barked, puppies yelped, and cats yowled. Though the shelter was always busy, it was currently bursting at the seams. Many animals had been injured and displaced as a result of the floods.

Most of the animals were housed in long corridors of concrete kennels. These kennels were designed for the short-term care of stray dogs, not for bears. The floor and three of the walls were made of cold, hard concrete, while the front of the cages were made from wire. For Georgia and Mollie the harsh and unwelcoming floor of the kennel was very different from the warm earth they had lazed on with their mother, and the soft bark of their favorite sleeping trees. Even Louisa, who could barely feel anything, noticed the hard rub of the concrete floor on her exposed, bony joints. However, the humans knew this would be safer for the cubs than the streets of Tbilisi.

Mollie and Georgia had already been placed in a kennel together. They huddled close to try and shield their ears from the howls and barks. They were terrified of humans and growled ferociously every time someone approached their kennel. When they were brought fresh fruit and bread they cowered at the back of the kennel, refusing to take the food until the humans were far out of sight.

When Louisa arrived, Mollie and Georgia sniffed the air. The smell was familiar. It was musty, like bear, but overpowered by all the other smells around. For a second Georgia wondered if it could be her mother. But it wasn't the smell of an adult bear; it was the smell of a bear cub, afraid and alone. What was this place? And why were young bears being brought here? She curled herself protectively around her sister. Whatever they were going to do to her, she would not let the humans hurt her or Mollie without a fight.

FACT FILE

Although it is important for bears to spend much of their day eating, they also do lots of sleeping! They make cozy spots to snuggle down for a daytime nap by trampling bushes or digging shallow pits into the ground. Some bears also climb trees and sleep there.

Some bears like to eat insects. These bears have a wide range of clever techniques for finding such delicious, crunchy snacks. They can turn over rocks, break open rotten logs, and dig in the earth with their long, strong front claws.

Louisa was placed in the kennel next door, alone, separated from Mollie and Georgia by a thick concrete wall. She still barely had the energy to move, but the team at the shelter were relieved to see her drinking fresh water from the bowl they had provided and eating a few small pieces of fruit. They silently wondered if she was beyond help, but vowed to do everything they could to save her.

Chapter Five

During the floods, lots of the animals from Tbilisi Zoo escaped from their enclosures and ran wild around the city. Many of these animals were trapped and injured in the rising water. The shelter tried to rescue as many animals as they could, but attempting to care for them was an enormous task.

In July 2015, representatives from UK charity, The Mayhew Animal Home, were visiting the Tbilisi Municipal Animal Shelter. The Mayhew came regularly to Tbilisi to help train the shelter vets, ensuring the best possible care for the rescued animals. For this visit, the CEO of The Mayhew Animal Home herself, Caroline Yates, had come to Tbilisi.

The Mayhew Animal Home is one of the most effective animal welfare organizations in London, helping thousands of dogs and cats escape lives of abandonment, cruelty, and neglect each year.

FACT FILE

When the team arrived, they were given a tour of the shelter. Every kennel was full, some containing more than four dogs. Extra crates had been erected in the passageways to house additional puppies and kittens. Everywhere they went they heard the sound of dogs, some cowering in the corner of their cage in fear. Some of the animals were still recovering from injuries sustained during the flood.

Kind-faced volunteers rushed around the place, doing the best they could to reassure and comfort the animals. But all of their supplies were running out, and there was not enough food or time to look after all the animals as they deserved.

At last the team from The Mayhew was led to an outside block, which housed the bear cubs. Dog barks still resonating in their ears, they spotted Mollie and Georgia, hunched in the furthest corner of their cage. Mollie's face was hidden in Georgia's thick fur, but Georgia's eyes and ears were just visible. Staring right at them, she looked terrified, but ready to attack anyone who came close enough to threaten her and her sister. The floor of their kennel was littered with breadcrumbs and their ragged blanket was ripped into useless shreds. It was a sorry sight. Two majestic mountain creatures, squatting, petrified, in a concrete kennel.

Bear claws are non-retractable. This means that unlike cat claws, bear claws always stick out. Bears use their claws for climbing, digging, and handling their food. You can see bears' claws in their tracks. Their front paws look like this:

FACT FILE

Next door, Louisa was close to the front of her cage, too weak to move away. She was still painfully thin, despite eating better. As the humans watched her, she began sucking her front paw. Her eyes were glazed, as if her mind was somewhere far away. Somewhere without dog barks and wire doors. Somewhere she could still snuggle into the warm embrace of her mother and brother. Somewhere she was free.

Paw sucking is sometimes seen in cubs that are separated from their mothers at a young age. It is a sign of stress. It is often associated with a vibrating hum, a noise which cubs usually make while suckling. In captivity, bear cubs suck their paws when they are frightened or need reassurance.

As soon as Caroline saw the bear cubs, she knew that something had to be done to help them and the shelter. Although the caretakers at the shelter were doing their best to look after the three girls, and they would certainly have died if they had not been rescued, this was no place for a bear cub to grow up. The wild that they had once known was fast fading into a distant memory.

Chapter Six

The search for the cubs' new home began immediately. Only the best sanctuary would be good enough. Everyone wanted them to feel grass beneath their feet, swim in a cool stream, and enjoy the shade of a leafy forest once more. In order to find the right home, Caroline called on the international wildlife charity, The Born Free Foundation.

There are currently around 450 wild bears living in Georgia and approximately the same number in Greece.

Born Free knew of a sanctuary in Greece, called Arcturos, that might be able to offer Mollie, Georgia, and Louisa all of these things. It was perfect! Arcturos was already home to seventeen bears and was located in the serene and majestic Verno mountains. Even the name "Arcturos" was perfect—it means "guardian of the bear." Born Free contacted the sanctuary to see if they had space for three more bear cubs. Everyone waited anxiously, fingers and toes crossed, to see what their answer would be.

The Born Free Foundation, an international wildlife charity devoted to compassionate conservation and animal welfare, was founded in 1985. They take action worldwide to protect threatened species and stop individual animal suffering, believing that wildlife belongs in the wild.

FACT FILE

Luckily, it was good news! Arcturos could provide the bears with a new home. But they did not yet have enough dens to provide the girls with a place to hibernate over the winter. Then there was the issue of transportation. Mollie, Georgia, and Louisa would have to travel over 1,500 miles (2,414 km) to reach Arcturos—and that would cost a lot of money.

Born Free were not discouraged by the great task of transferring the cubs all the way from their kennels in Georgia to the green mountains of Greece. The Born Free team are experts at arranging lifesaving trips for animals in trouble, and this one would be no different!

Together with The Mayhew Animal Home and with support from The Mail on Sunday and popstar Mollie King, Born Free began to raise all the funds they needed. There was a lot to save for: feeding the bears healthy food while they remained in the shelter, building them some temporary dens to keep them warm, organizing a mountain of paperwork to move them from one country to another, chartering a plane to fly them from Georgia to Greece, and modifying special crates for transporting them! Before the cubs could travel, they also needed to be checked over by Born Free's head veterinarian, Dr. John Knight.

The study of bears is called Ursology. Someone who studies bears is called an ursologist.

FACT FILE

Chapter Seven

Dr. John, along with other members of the Born Free team, arrived in Tbilisi as the city was beginning to recover from the devastation of the floods. Its residents had been very busy. Much of the damage had already been repaired and people were beginning to carry on with life as normal.

Though the shelter was less busy now and there were fewer dogs crammed into the corridors, the sound of barking was still overwhelming. But the bear cubs were doing well. Mollie and Georgia were becoming less frightened of humans. As Dr. John approached their kennel, Georgia came to the door to greet him, hoping he might have brought her some food. She was in luck! He passed her a banana through the wire, which she grabbed hastily, then retreated to a far corner. Mollie's eyes were locked on the apple in his other hand, but she was still more cautious. Dr. John rolled the apple under the door toward her. She grabbed it and shuffled backwards, keeping her eyes on this unfamiliar human at all times.

Bears help to distribute and fertilize new plants by transporting the seeds of the fruit they eat through their droppings (also called scat).

Louisa, on the other hand, longed for company. She would try to climb onto the caretakers' laps whenever they brought her food, desperate for cuddles and comfort. She missed playing with her brother and snuggling into her mother's soft, dense fur. She longed for another bear cub to play with. She often wondered about the sounds and smells she had heard from the kennel beside her. She knew there were bear cubs there and that they were both girls, similar in age to her. There was no adult with them though. Were these bear cubs also orphaned in the floods? Were they as lonely as she was? She had no way to see them, but could still smell and hear them. Sometimes, she would close her eyes, suck on her paw, and pretend the scent and sounds were her family.

Louisa had put on a little more weight, but was still painfully thin. The team were very worried about her. They told Dr. John that when she was alone, Louisa was sucking her paw more than ever. He soon got to work checking the bear cubs over. He looked at their eyes, ears, and teeth. He watched them walk and listened to their hearts. He confirmed that they were all girls and talked to the team about the cubs' behavior and eating habits. He even looked at the bears' poo! After a very thorough clinical examination, Dr. John had finally reached a verdict.

Most bears have 42 teeth. All of their adult teeth should be in place by the time they are two and a half years old.

It was bad news. The bear cubs were still too underweight and malnourished to endure the arduous 1,500 mile (2,414 km) journey to their new home in Greece. Louisa needed to put on a lot more weight and all three bears needed to be treated for worms. Everyone was very sad and disappointed. The top priority now was to do everything they could to get the cubs healthy enough to make the trip.

FACT FILE

Bears can suffer from over fifty types of parasitic worm, all of which can weaken them and make them more likely to get other diseases or die from starvation.

Dr. John treated all three cubs for internal parasites, which may have been preventing the bears from putting on as much weight as they needed to. He advised the shelter on what food the cubs needed to grow strong enough for their grueling journey. He suggested that they be given fish, nuts, berries, and honey alongside the bread and fruit they already received daily. As well as bringing them some special balls, called Boomer balls, to play with, he also taught the team how to hide the bears' favorite food inside toys and logs, to keep their brains active.

FACT FILE

As they were not yet ready to travel, Mollie, Georgia, and Louisa would have to spend the winter in Tbilisi. The wonderful team at the animal shelter used some of the money raised by The Mayhew to build special, cozy winter dens for the bears to spend the coldest months in. The cubs seemed content enough as they settled down for winter. They were getting used to life in Tbilisi and though the conditions were far from ideal, they would at least remain warm and safe. And a good thing too, because when spring came, there would be a big adventure waiting for them!

FACT FILE

There are lots of dangers for a bear cub in the wild. Predators such as wolves, big cats, and even adult male bears will kill and eat baby bears. Bear cubs that don't find enough to eat may starve to death. Some also die from disease and accidental falls. But the biggest threat of all to bears, whether young or old, is humans.

Chapter Eight

Months passed and winter slowly thawed. As the temperatures began to rise in Tbilisi, Georgia started pacing her small cage. She longed to roam in the mountains and laze in the quiet shade of a big, leafy tree. There was no space to play in her small kennel and she was desperate to stretch her legs, which had grown significantly over the winter.

Dogs and cats walk up on their tiptoes; this is called digitigrade walking. Bears, however, walk like humans, with their heels on the ground; this is called plantigrade walking.

FACT FILE

Though Georgia did not know it, she would not be waiting much longer. Dr. John had confirmed that all three bears were now healthy enough to travel. With this news the Born Free team jumped into action. They shipped the travel crates to Georgia and chartered a special plane to fly the cubs to Greece. The final piece of the puzzle was for the Georgian government to grant a special export license for the movement of the three bears. On May 13, 2016, Mollie, Georgia, and Louisa would be on their way to their new home!

The journey would start at Tbilisi International Airport, where they would board a plane in their crates and take a four-hour flight to Thessaloniki International Airport in northern Greece. There the team from Arcturos, along with the Born Free rescue team, would greet them with a huge truck in which they would continue their journey. They would then travel west in the truck for another three hours, climbing the forested Verno mountains, before finally reaching Arcturos Bear Sanctuary late that afternoon. At every step, Dr. John would be keeping an eye on the bears to make sure they were happy and healthy.

Some species of bears have been found at altitudes of more than 3 mi (5,000 m).

Finally, the day came. Everyone was up even before the crack of dawn, excited and nervous about the bear cubs' journey but also sad to say goodbye. All the volunteers had become very attached to the cubs during their time at the shelter.

When the transport team arrived, Georgia, Mollie, and Louisa were fast asleep! Waking up, they looked at the people with their heads cocked to one side. It was far too early for breakfast! The team's first task was to move the bears into individual transport crates, which were actually designed for leopards but were the perfect size for the bear cubs. When the humans came to the door of their kennel, Mollie and Georgia realized that something strange was happening. A huge box was pushed up to the door of their kennel and there were lots more people around than normal. Some of them were even taking photographs.

These new boxes, which were even smaller and darker than the kennels, were very frightening. Dr. John tried his hardest to coax Georgia out of her kennel, knowing that she was the bravest, by showing her a honey and apple treat that the team had specially prepared. Eventually, the temptation of the sweet smell overcame her fear and she crept into the box.

As soon as she had walked fully into the transport crate, the door was dropped and she was trapped inside. In the kennel, Mollie started to panic. She had never been separated from her sister before. After losing her mother in the forest, the fear of losing her sister as well was unbearable. Georgia grunted to Mollie, letting her know that she was okay.

Mollie was easier to tempt into the crate. Having watched her sister go into one, she did not want to be left in the kennel alone! Louisa was the easiest of all; she would do anything for a little bit of attention. Once they were all safely secured in their crates, the three bears were transferred to Tbilisi Airport, a short journey from the shelter. As they left, they peered out of the front of their crates, swiveling their ears, trying to make sense of what was happening. For the first time since their rescues, the incessant barking of dogs was replaced with the whining sounds of machinery.

Bears can move their ears to locate where sounds are coming from.

The next big task was to secure the crates within the plane. It was a small, yellow and blue cargo plane, chartered from Greece especially to transport the three bear cubs. As the travel crates were so heavy, a forklift truck was needed to move them into the hold.

The team watched carefully as the crates slid into the plane. Everyone knew that this must be an unnerving experience, but Mollie, Georgia, and Louisa were very brave and accepted it all without complaint.

FACT FILE

European brown bears are generally much smaller than those found in the Americas, averaging weights of around 485 lbs (220 kg) for an adult male. The Kodiak bear in Alaska, another subspecies of brown bear, can weigh up to 1,720 lbs (780 kg)!

As the engines started, the bear cubs looked around with interest. The plane doors closed onto the only human faces they had grown to know and trust and they suddenly felt very alone—especially Mollie, separated from Georgia, whom she relied upon for comfort and security. The bear cubs did not understand what was causing this new strange noise or why they were leaving Tbilisi.

Soon, they were in the air, and though they were still frightened and confused, the whirring sounds of the plane eventually sent the cubs to sleep. As they dozed in their travel crates, the cubs soared across the border of Georgia and over the width of Turkey, crossed the Aegean Sea and eventually descended into northern Greece. After landing, the doors of the plane opened and the bears got their first glimpse of the country they would now call home forever. Hot, dry air rushed in and tickled the cubs' nostrils with delicious new smells. The musky bear smell, which had filled the plane, was replaced with the hot, salty scent of the sea. The bears were thankful for the feel of the cool floor of their travel crates against their paws.

A bear's fur is great at keeping them warm in the winter, but in the summer, it can make them very hot! Bears mainly regulate their temperature through the hairless skin on their paws, which has a rich blood supply to carry cooled blood to the rest of the body.

There was a huge truck waiting for them on the runway. It had "ARCTUROS" written in big letters across the front and a large, covered back, which was perfect to protect the bears from the baking Greek sun. It was a three-hour drive to the sanctuary, so after the customs paperwork was completed everyone stopped for some lunch. The bears were given a meal of apples, bananas, and some freshly baked Greek bread. Dr. John also offered them more fresh, cold water, which they lapped up gratefully, spilling it all over the bottom of their crates.

When lunch was over they began the final stretch of their journey. The trip reminded Mollie and Georgia of being taken to the shelter in Tbilisi, all those months ago, just days after losing their mother. Where were they being taken this time? The kennel in Tbilisi was neither comfortable nor comforting, but at least they had been safe there and the humans had been kind. This journey was leading to somewhere completely unknown. Mollie let out a small cry, to which Georgia replied with a grunt. Mollie relaxed a little. As long as she was with her sister, she knew she would be okay.

Near the end of the journey, the road became a little steeper. Louisa, who had fallen asleep, rolled to the edge of her crate and woke with a start. She began to suck her paw. She wished her mother was there to comfort her. At last, they arrived at the gates of the

Arcturos Bear Sanctuary's nursery and quarantine area. The road was flanked by the tall, thin trunks of young beech trees and coal tits (black-crested birds) called from their nests.

Adult male bears are called boars.
Adult female bears are called sows.

Chapter Nine

The big truck trundled through the gates of the nursery, where the cubs could be released into their temporary enclosure, only 20 minutes from the main 17 ac^2 (7 ha) woodland that would later become their permanent home. Soon the frightening journey would all be worth it.

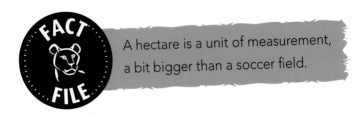

FACT FILE

A hectare is a unit of measurement, a bit bigger than a soccer field.

At first, the cubs would only be allowed in a small medical pen, so that it would be easy to catch them if there were any problems. Then, if everything went well, they would be introduced to a much larger quarantine enclosure, where they would stay until the center team was sure that they were not carrying any diseases and that they were settled and independent enough for life in the main sanctuary.

When animals are moved to new countries or their history is unknown, they are put into quarantine before being allowed to interact with others of their species. This is to prevent the spread of illness and disease.

FACT FILE

Georgia was the first out, tentatively stepping into the bright Greek sunlight. One of the greatest shocks was the silence. After almost a year of living amid the barking cacophony of a dog shelter, her ears still ringing from the rumble of the truck, Georgia finally felt at peace. After a few steps, feeling the dry, soft earth beneath her paws and the warmth of the sun beating onto her back, she galloped around in a big circle, and then threw herself onto the floor. The Arcturos team had scattered apples and honey on the sun-baked ground as a treat and to encourage the cubs to explore their new home. Georgia rolled around in joy, pressing her aching shoulders hard into the earth, stretching out her legs and licking up the honey.

Adult bears mark their territories by rubbing their scent onto trees, either by stretching out and scratching their backs or biting and clawing the bark.

FACT FILE

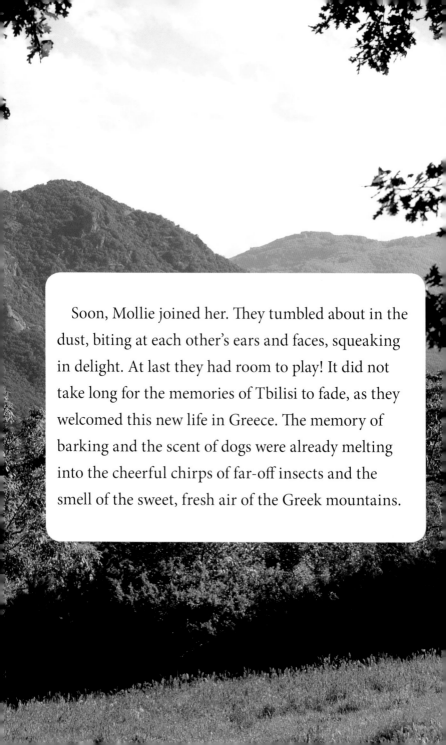

Soon, Mollie joined her. They tumbled about in the dust, biting at each other's ears and faces, squeaking in delight. At last they had room to play! It did not take long for the memories of Tbilisi to fade, as they welcomed this new life in Greece. The memory of barking and the scent of dogs were already melting into the cheerful chirps of far-off insects and the smell of the sweet, fresh air of the Greek mountains.

Playing is more than just a game to bear cubs; it teaches them to fight and hunt. It also teaches them how to read the body language of other bears and when to be submissive.

Then it was time for Mollie and Georgia to meet Louisa. Everyone was a little bit nervous. Bears will sometimes fight if they feel uncertain or threatened. Normally, bear cubs learn how to interact in social situations from their mother. None of the orphaned bear cubs had received these lessons, so it was hard to predict how they would react.

Despite living so close for so long and smelling each other every day, this was the first time that Mollie, Georgia, and Louisa would be able to see each other. Everyone expected Louisa to be overjoyed at having company at last, but were worried that Mollie and Georgia might be aggressive toward her. In the wild, bear cubs rarely interact with other bears that are not part of their direct family. Dr. John suggested that the sisters be introduced to Louisa one by one, so they would not gang up on her.

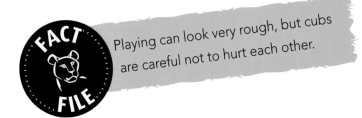

FACT FILE

Playing can look very rough, but cubs are careful not to hurt each other.

Georgia was first, as she was the bravest. When the doors opened, the cubs stood still, neither knowing what to do. For Louisa, it was the first time she had seen another bear since losing her mother and brother. She had lived next to Georgia for so long, but now that the time had come, she had forgotten how to play. She lowered her head and pulled her small ears down onto her skull. She did not want any trouble. Both bear cubs were trying to decide if the other cub was a threat. Louisa yawned, trying to show Georgia that she was not interested in causing a fight.

A lot of bear communication happens through body language—the way they move their head, ears, mouth, and body.

FACT FILE

Eventually, Georgia walked over to Louisa, sniffing her all over. All of the muscles in Louisa's body stiffened. Louisa could not believe it! It really was that bear cub that she had been living beside for all this time! She was not a danger. They were kindred spirits, sharing that strange experience of living in the shelter, then traveling thousands of miles to their new Greek home.

Georgia tried to encourage Louisa to play, but Louisa was too scared. She backed off and sniffed the earth, hoping that Georgia would get the message. Georgia took the hint, and instead turned her attention to the rescue team and photographers, who had been silently watching and documenting the whole spectacle from the other side of the fence. She leaped toward them, curious to see what they were doing.

Though the team had hoped that the cubs may make friends, they always knew that it would be a slow process. Most of all, they were very relieved that Georgia had not been aggressive. Next, it was Mollie's turn. She was just as shy as Louisa. They circled each other, bodies low to the ground, sniffing the air and stealing shy glances every few seconds. As the circles drew tighter, they were finally within touching distance. This time, it was Louisa that made first contact, reaching out her long snout to sniff Mollie's rump.

The team held their breath, hoping that Mollie could convince Louisa to play. Louisa rolled on the floor, showing Mollie her belly and inviting her to wrestle. The team watched excitedly—at last Louisa would have a friend! Then, suddenly, and much to everyone's disappointment, Mollie turned her back on Louisa and walked away. Louisa rolled onto her side and started to suck her paw.

It was not the instant friendship that everyone had dreamed of, but at least the cubs would tolerate each other. They had plenty of time to become friends and most importantly, they had arrived safely in their beautiful new mountain home.

Chapter Ten

After a few days settling into the sounds and smells of their holding pen, Mollie, Georgia, and Louisa were becoming accustomed to Greek life. The weather was beautiful, the food was delicious, and the team was gentle and kind. Mollie and Georgia still largely ignored Louisa and played alone, but after the initial rejection, Louisa was too afraid to try and join them. Despite this, she was much happier than she had been in the kennel in Tbilisi and passed her days rolling in the dry earth and watching the sisters chase each other around the pen.

As they were doing so well, the Arcturos team decided that the girls were ready to be released into their quarantine enclosure. It was much bigger than the holding pen, with large swathes of grass, mounds to climb, and tree trunks to scratch. They loped about, sniffing every plant and log, grunting excitedly to each other. The grass felt soft and springy under their feet and the earth smelled sweet and fresh. The girls were so distracted by all of these incredible new sensations that they almost failed to notice that there was already another bear in this enclosure—Patrick.

In Greece, mother bears were often killed so that their cubs could be stolen and sold as dancing bears. These poor cubs had their noses and lips pierced with rings so that their handlers could control them. They often had all of their teeth smashed out so that they posed less of a threat. And they were made to stand on hot metal plates to force them to move their hind feet in a shuffle that looked like they were dancing.

Like Mollie, Georgia, and Louisa, Patrick was an orphan. He was found alone, not far from the Arcturos Bear Sanctuary. It is likely that his mother was killed by a car, leaving Patrick all alone. Patrick was just a couple of months older than the female cubs and, until the new cubs arrived, he had lived alone in this enclosure. Everyone hoped that he would welcome the company of the three new cubs and not become protective of his territory.

They need not have worried. It immediately became clear that Patrick had found a new best friend. While Mollie and Georgia hung around by the edges of the enclosure, hoping for humans to visit and share a tasty treat of fruit and honey with them, Louisa ran straight up to Patrick and pounced on him! Maybe this male cub reminded her of her brother, perhaps she had learned something from her introductions to Mollie and Georgia, or maybe it was just a random moment of bravery. Whatever caused it, they have been inseparable ever since. Even when Patrick is fast asleep, snoring loudly, Louisa will curl up next to him, her head on his shaggy back.

As Mollie, Georgia, Louisa, and Patrick were orphaned at such a young age, they missed crucial lessons from their mothers about how to survive in the wild. They are also totally reliant on humans for food, and have lost their natural fear of people. For these reasons, the cubs will never be able to live completely wild lives and will stay at Arcturos forever. Fortunately, this sanctuary in the middle of the European wilderness is about as close to a wild life as they could get!

Bears and wolves are sometimes shot by sheep farmers in Greece, who blame them for killing and eating their sheep.

FACT FILE

All of the bears at Arcturos Bear Sanctuary have had troubled starts to their lives. Some came from terrible zoos, others were rescued from lives of dancing on the streets, and some had even been kept as pets. They now all live together in an enormous forest enclosure, where they will be kept healthy and safe for the rest of their lives. As they are so young, Mollie, Georgia, Louisa, and Patrick will stay in their quarantine enclosure through the winter months. Then, in the spring, the team hopes that they will be ready to move into the bear forest.

Chapter Eleven

In the serene mountain sanctuary, as the leaves turn red and gold, the four young bear cubs have made themselves at home. It is often possible to spot Louisa and Patrick's tracks snaking across their enclosure. Running side by side, their paw marks reveal hours of mischievous exploring. His prints, bigger and deeper than hers, are always slightly ahead. He clearly leads the adventures!

FACT FILE

A bear's tracks are like its fingerprint. Distinguishing features include sole cracks and broken claws. A good tracker can tell the age, weight, and sex of a bear just by looking at its tracks.

Large, flattened areas of vegetation give away Mollie and Georgia's favorite pastime. They love nothing more than rolling around in the lush, green grass, especially after lunch, when their bellies are full of a delicious feast of meats and fruits.

In the wild, bear cubs leave their mothers and choose their own place to live at about three or four years of age. However, with the threat of poaching and vast areas of their natural habitat facing deforestation, there are few safe places left for bears to call their own.

While the wild forests of the world are still the best place for brown bears, these four little orphans are lucky. Their beech wood sanctuary will provide them with a safe place to live healthy and happy lives.

Thanks to the hard work of some very kind people, Mollie, Georgia, Louisa, and Patrick will call the bear forest home for the rest of their days.

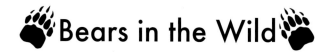 Bears in the Wild

Polar Bear

These enormous white bears live on Arctic sea ice in one of the world's coldest environments. They have a thick layer of fat and fur to keep them warm and their front paws are partially webbed to help them swim through the icy waters.

Polar bear statistics:

- Estimated polar bear population: 22,000–31,000
- Lives throughout the ice-covered waters of the circumpolar Arctic
- Population status: vulnerable

What threatens polar bears?

The increase in global temperatures is causing the ice sheets on which polar bears hunt for seals to shrink rapidly. With nowhere left to hunt, the southernmost polar bear populations are decreasing.

American Black Bear

Native to the forests of North America, the American black bear is much smaller than the brown bear and has a shorter and darker coat. It is the world's most common species of bear.

American black bear statistics:

- Estimated American black bear population: 850,000–950,000
- Lives across North America
- Population status: least concern

What threatens wild American black bears?

American black bears are legally hunted for sport, meat, and fur across the U.S. and Canada. They are also losing large areas of their habitat to human developments and roads.

Asiatic Black Bear

Also known as the moon bear because of the moon-shaped white patch on its chest, this species has a shaggy black coat, which extends into a thick mane around its neck.

Asiatic black bear statistics:

🐾 Estimated Asiatic black bear population: unknown, estimates range from 36,000–76,000

🐾 Lives in southern and eastern Asia

🐾 Population status: vulnerable

What threatens wild Asiatic black bears?

The biggest threat to Asiatic black bears is the bear bile industry. In traditional Chinese medicine, bear bile is used to treat disease. Bile is obtained from the bear's gall bladder. It is thought that over 12,000 bears are currently being farmed for bear bile.

Brown Bear

Brown bears are found in more places across the globe than any other species of bear. Brown bears can be identified by their large size and the hump of muscle over their shoulders.

Brown bear statistics:

🐾 Estimated worldwide brown bear population: more than 200,000

🐾 Lives in northern North America, Europe, and Asia

🐾 Population status: least concern

What threatens wild brown bears?

In Europe, brown bears are in serious trouble. There is very little natural wilderness remaining. Brown bears are often illegally hunted and sometimes their cubs are taken to zoos, circuses, or to be used as dancing bears.

Giant Panda

The giant panda is known worldwide for its striking black and white coat and gentle temperament. They feed almost exclusively on bamboo and spend almost all of their waking hours eating.

Giant panda statistics

- Estimated worldwide giant panda population: 1,000–2,000
- Lives in Western China
- Population status: vulnerable

What threatens wild giant pandas?

Conversion of high altitude bamboo forest into farmland has restricted the areas available for giant pandas and has isolated patches of bamboo forest. It is therefore difficult for giant pandas to find new places to live or food to eat.

Sloth Bear

The sloth bear is the only bear species to primarily feed on insects. To help it with this specialized diet, the sloth bear has long, highly mobile lips, and curved claws for digging.

Sloth bear statistics

- Estimated worldwide sloth bear population: approximately 20,000
- Lives in India, Nepal, Sri Lanka, and Bhutan
- Population status: vulnerable

What threatens wild sloth bears?

Sloth bears face a wide range of threats. They are losing habitat due to the expansion of human settlements and roads. Adult sloth bears are also poached for the use of their bones, teeth, and claws in medicines, and as lucky charms.

Sun Bear

The sun bear is the smallest of all the bear species. It spends most of its time in trees and loves to eat honey. It has an incredibly long tongue to help it extract honey from beehives. Every sun bear has its own individually patterned chest patch.

Sun bear statistics

- Estimated worldwide sun bear population: unknown
- Lives in Southeast Asia, China, India, and Bangladesh
- Population status: vulnerable

What threatens wild sun bears?

Sun bears face three main threats: habitat loss, commercial hunting, and the pet trade. As the smallest bear in the world, some people mistakenly think sun bears will make cute pets. Sun bear cubs are stolen from their mothers and taken into captivity, where they often die due to inadequate care.

Spectacled Bear

The spectacled bear is the only species of bear to live in South America. It has a short face, which is often covered in yellow and white patterns. The mountains where they live are very remote, so little is known about them.

Spectacled bear statistics

- Estimated worldwide spectacled bear population: unknown
- Lives in Bolivia, Colombia, Ecuador, Peru, and Venezuela
- Population status: vulnerable

What threatens wild spectacled bears?

Spectacled bears are hunted for their skin, claws, fat, meat, and bile, which are all sold on the black market. Spectacled bears are also losing their habitat due to mining, road development, agriculture, and oil exploitation.

Read all the rescue stories

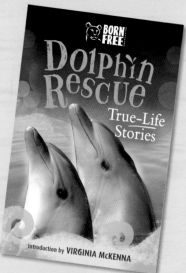

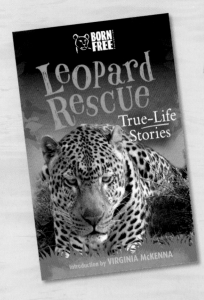

Keep Wildlife in the Wild

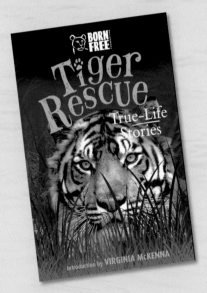

Tiger
Rescue
True-Life
Stories

Introduction by VIRGINIA McKENNA

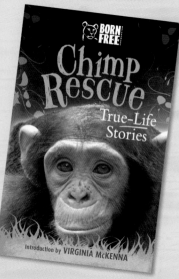

Chimp
Rescue
True-Life
Stories

Introduction by VIRGINIA McKENNA

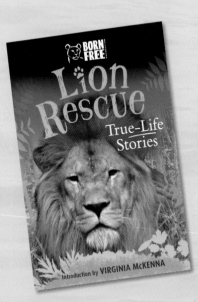

Lion
Rescue
True-Life
Stories

Introduction by VIRGINIA McKENNA

BARRON'S

Go wild with Born Free

Welcome to the Born Free Foundation, where people get into animals and go wild! Our wildlife charity takes action all around the world to save lions, elephants, gorillas, tigers, chimps, dolphins, bears, wolves, and lots more.

If you're wild about animals, visit
www.bornfreeusa.org
To join our free kids' club, WildcreW, or adopt your own animal, visit
www.bornfree.org.uk

Keep Wildlife in the Wild